CONTENTS

Power house
◆ 16 ◆

The big push
◆ 18 ◆

Neat work
◆ 20 ◆

Branching out
◆ 22 ◆

Feel the force
◆ 24 ◆

Pole to pole
◆ 26 ◆

Magnetic art
◆ 28 ◆

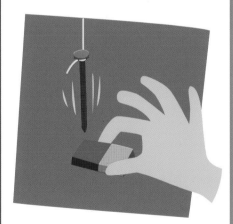

Make your own magnets
◆ 30 ◆

Mini-magnets
◆ 32 ◆

Map it out
◆ 34 ◆

Pick-up power
◆ 36 ◆

Glossary
◆ 38 ◆

Index
◆ 40 ◆

Getting started

Every time we switch on a light or turn on the TV, we are using electricity. When we close the fridge door or play a tape, we use magnetism. If you've ever wanted to know what electricity and magnetism are, how they work and how we use them, then this is the book for you. It is packed with activities and things to make. Before you start, read these pages carefully – they give you lots of useful advice. A few minutes' reading now could save you hours of bother later!

Are you well connected?

If you try the electrical activities on pages 10-37, you'll find electricity only flows between things that are properly stuck together. So when you build a circuit, make sure it has really good connections.

Ask an adult to strip the plastic off the ends of your plastic-coated wires. Electricity can only flow through the bare metal – it does not flow through plastic

Fix a wire to the terminals of a battery with sticky tape or modelling clay. Make sure the metal part of the wire touches the metal part of the battery.

The right stuff

To try out most of the activities in the book, you only need a few everyday things like batteries, spoons, lemons and paper clips. Sometimes, you'll need more unusual items like iron filings, wire wool and mini-lightbulbs. Try your local toy or hobby shop for these.

Mini-lightbulbs that screw in to a base like this are the easiest sort to use, or you can use bulbs without a base.

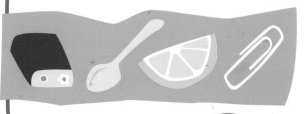

For most of the activities, any small battery will do. Put it in a radio to make sure it isn't flat!

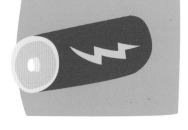

You will also need several lengths of plastic-coated (insulated) wire.

Try to get two straight bar magnets like this.

HANDS-ON
Science

...nd Magnets

Sarah Angliss

Illustrations by David Le Jars

KINGFISHER

KINGFISHER
Kingfisher Publications Plc
New Penderel House,
283–288 High Holborn,
London WC1V 7HZ
www.kingfisherpub.com

Produced for Kingfisher by PAGE*One*
Cairn House, Elgiva Lane, Chesham
Buckinghamshire HP5 2JD

For PAGE*One*
Creative Director Bob Gordon
Project Editor Miriam Richardson
Designers Monica Bratt, Tim Stansfield

Illustrator David Le Jars

For Kingfisher
Managing Editor Clive Wilson
Production Manager Oonagh Phelan
DTP Co-ordinator Nicky Studdart

First published by Kingfisher Publications Plc 2001
10 9 8 7 6 5 4 3
3TR/0906/TIMS/GRST/157MA/C

A CIP catalogue record for this book is available from
the British Library

ISBN: 978 0 7534 0270 2

Printed in China

Getting started
◆ 4 ◆

What a tingle!
◆ 6 ◆

Make it move
◆ 8 ◆

Wire it up
◆ 10 ◆

Thick and thin
◆ 12 ◆

Go with the flow
◆ 14 ◆

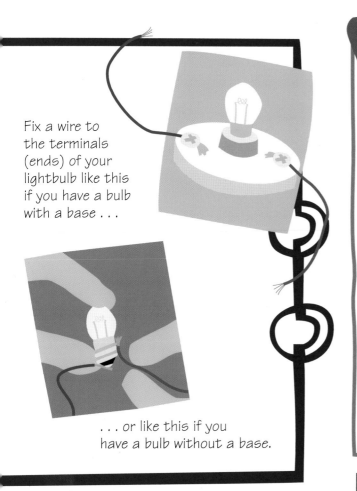

Fix a wire to the terminals (ends) of your lightbulb like this if you have a bulb with a base . . .

. . . or like this if you have a bulb without a base.

Warning

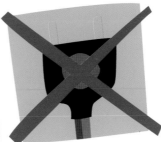

The electrical activities in this book use small batteries that give off very little electricity.

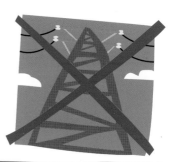

Never experiment with mains electricity (the sort that comes out of plugs and sockets at home or school). It is thousands of times more powerful than a small battery. It can kill.

Never play near overhead pylons or electricity substations. Even when you're not touching them, electricity can jump from them and kill you.

Stuck for words?

If you come across a word you don't understand, or you just want to find out a bit more, have a look in the Glossary on pages 38 and 39.

Clock symbol

The clock symbol at the start of each experiment shows you approximately how many minutes the activity should take. All the experiments take between 5 and 30 minutes. If you are using glue allow extra time for drying.

10

Having problems?

Don't worry if you have trouble with some of the activities in this book.

If things don't seem to be working, read through each step of the activity again, then have another go.

Remember, even the greatest scientists had problems with their experiments. Take J J Thompson, for example, the scientist who discovered the electron. He was so clumsy, his students would never let him go near his own equipment!

What a tingle!

Electricity, is a form of energy – it makes things happen. For instance, it can heat up a toaster or light up a bulb. We usually think of electricity as something that flows through wires. But there's another form of electricity that doesn't flow at all, called 'static electricity'. You can make this by rubbing certain things together, which gives one or other of them something called 'charge'.

FLASHBACK

Bright sparks

The Ancient Greeks discovered static electricity over 2,000 years ago. They realised that amber, a fossilised tree sap, would pick up feathers after it was rubbed with silk. Our words 'electricity' and 'electron' (see right) come from the Greek word 'elektra', which means 'amber'.

Snake charmer

Use static electricity to move things with no hands! Make sure everything you use in these activities is dry.

YOU WILL NEED
10
◆ TISSUE PAPER
◆ A PLASTIC RULER
◆ A SCRAP OF NYLON FABRIC
◆ SCISSORS

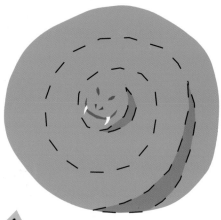

1 Copy this pattern on to the tissue paper and cut it out. Cut along the dotted line, then pull one end to make a spiralling snake. Make more snakes to go with it.

2 Rub a plastic ruler several times with a scrap of nylon.

3 Wave the ruler close to your snakes. Can you lift them up without touching them?

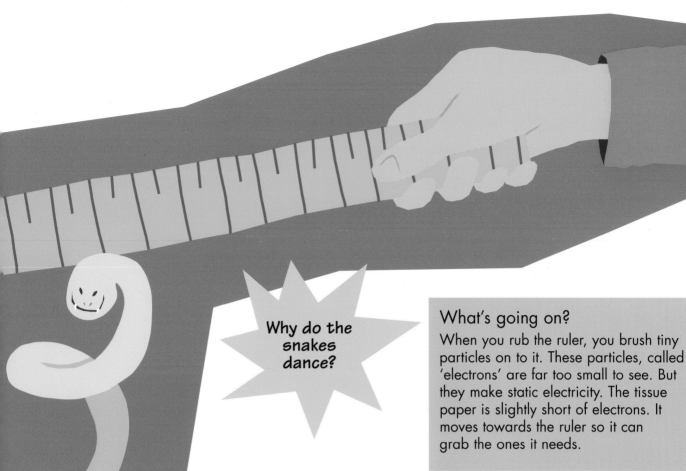

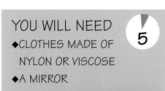

Why do the snakes dance?

What's going on?

When you rub the ruler, you brush tiny particles on to it. These particles, called 'electrons' are far too small to see. But they make static electricity. The tissue paper is slightly short of electrons. It moves towards the ruler so it can grab the ones it needs.

Fashion victim

Listen carefully while you take off some nylon or viscose clothes. If it's dark, look into a mirror while you do this. Do you hear tiny crackles, or see tiny sparks?

YOU WILL NEED
- CLOTHES MADE OF NYLON OR VISCOSE
- A MIRROR

5

What's going on?

The crackles you hear and sparks you see when you take off the clothes are caused by electrons on the move, between your body and your clothes. They are just like mini thunder and lightning!

ELECTRIC STORM
If enough charge builds up in a cloud, it may release itself suddenly in a bolt of lightning. The heat of the lightning makes the air expand, creating a crash of thunder.

Make it move!

An object tends not to keep its charge. If possible, it will dump it on other things nearby. You can make use of this to make things move. Objects attract (pull towards each other) if they have an opposite charge. This lets them get close enough to share electrons so their charge will go away. If they have the same charge, they can't dump electrons on each other and they 'repel' (push each other apart).

What makes the butterfly's wings move?

It's alive!

Charge up a delicate paper butterfly to bring it to life.

YOU WILL NEED
- A METAL PAPER CLIP
- AN EMPTY JAM JAR
- MODELLING CLAY
- KITCHEN FOIL
- TISSUE PAPER
- A PLASTIC RULER
- A SCRAP OF NYLON
- SCISSORS

20

1 Uncurl your paper clip. Then bend it into the shape you can see in this picture.

2 Take a scrap of kitchen foil, about the size of the palm of your hand, and roll it into a tight ball. Poke the end of your paper clip into the ball of foil.

3 Rest your paper clip on the rim of the jar, using a piece of modelling clay to keep it in place. Cut a tiny butterfly out of tissue paper. Lay it on your paper clip, inside the jar.

4 Rub a plastic ruler with a scrap of nylon. This will charge it up (see pages 6–7). Watch the butterfly carefully as you bring the ruler very close to the foil ball. Can you see the butterfly's wings move?

What's going on?

The charged ruler has lots of extra electrons which it wants to dump on other objects around it. It can do this when you bring it close to the ball. Electrons find it easy to move through metal so they flow through the ball and paper clip, into the paper. As they give both wings of the butterfly the same charge, the wings repel each other – they open up.

In the bag

Cut a strip from the bag and rub it with the scrap of nylon. This will charge it up by giving it extra electrons. Then rub each of your other objects in turn. Bring them close to the charged plastic strip. If they have lost electrons, they have an opposite charge to the strip so they will be attracted towards it. If they have gained electrons, they will have the same charge as the strip so they will be repelled by it.

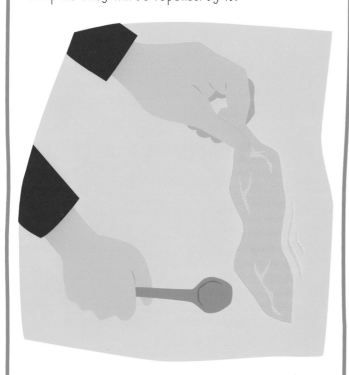

What's going on?
When you rub them, plastic objects, such as the ballpoint pen casing, gain electrons. That's why they repel the strip. Metal objects, such as the fork, lose electrons so they attract the strip. A few objects, including the eraser, do very little to the strip because they hardly pick up any charge at all.

Hair raising

Something has 'charge' when it gains or loses electrons. A thing that has gained electrons will have an opposite charge to something that has lost them. What happens when you charge up your hair by repeatedly passing a plastic comb through it?

What's going on?
The comb brushes electrons on to your hair. It gives every one of your hairs the same type of charge. As the hairs can't dump their extra charge on each other, they stand on end to keep themselves apart.

AIRSHIP FIRE
In May 1937, the huge *Hindenburg* airship went up in flames when the crew threw some ropes to the ground. They hadn't realised that the weather was stormy and lots of charge had built up on the ship's outer shell. This charge flowed along the ropes, into the ground, causing a spark that set the gas inside the airship alight.

Wire it up

So far, you've only experimented with static electricity – the kind that's made when you brush electrons on to things or rub electrons off them. However, there's another very useful type of electricity that's made by electrons on the move. It's called 'current electricity'. Electrons find it easy to move through metal. Using a battery, you can push them all the way through a metal wire. To do this, you need to make the wire into a complete loop, called a 'circuit', that lets them flow out of the battery then in again.

Bright idea

When current electricity flows through this circuit, it lights up a bulb.

YOU WILL NEED
10
◆ A SMALL TORCH BULB (WITH A MAXIMUM VOLTAGE OF 3V OR 4.5V)
◆ A 1.5V AA-SIZE BATTERY
◆ TWO INSULATED WIRES
◆ STICKY TAPE

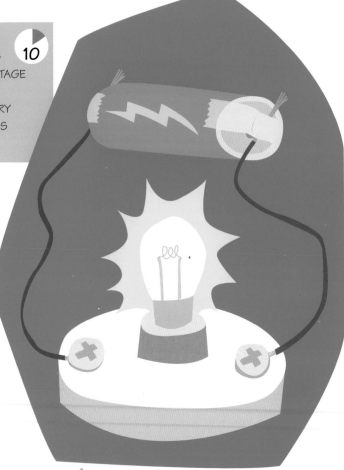

1 Ask an adult to strip around 2cm of plastic from each end of your wires.

2 Using sticky tape, fix the bare end of one wire to the silvery knob on the top of your battery. This knob is called the 'positive terminal'.

4 Connect your two free ends of wire to the lightbulb. Does your bulb glow?

3 Using some more tape, fix the bare end of your other wire to the silvery base of your battery. This is called the 'negative terminal'.

What's going on?
You have a made a complete circuit. Electrons can flow out of the battery, through one wire, through the bulb, through the other wire then into the battery again. When they flow through the bulb, they make it glow.

Bridge the gap

Follow the steps in 'Bright idea' (left) again to make your torch bulb glow. Ask an adult to cut one of your wires in half to break the circuit. Keep everything else in place. Now ask your adult helper to strip the two free ends of broken wire. Then, using a metal paper clip, touch both free ends of bare wire at the same time. What happens to the bulb?

What happens to the bulb when you break your circuit?

10

YOU WILL NEED

- A SMALL TORCH BULB (WITH A MAXIMUM VOLTAGE OF 3V OR 4.5V)
- A 1.5V AA-SIZE BATTERY
- TWO INSULATED WIRES
- A METAL PAPER CLIP
- STICKY TAPE

What's going on?

When you break the circuit, electricity can't flow all the way round it so the bulb stops glowing. The metal paper clip can bridge the gap in the broken circuit. When you press it against the two bare ends of broken wire, electricity can flow through it, from one piece of wire to the other. The paper clip completes the circuit, letting the bulb glow. In this way, it works as a switch.

FLASHBACK

Say it with lights

Electricity came into homes at the end of the nineteenth century. At that time, it was an expensive luxury, only seen in the richest city addresses. Electric light was so costly, people only put it in their most important rooms. Some people who could afford only one lightbulb decided to put it in the hall. They left their only electric light on all day – even when they were out – to show it off to passers-by.

PINBALL

The steel ball in this pinball machine bridges the gap between the target and base of the machine. This completes a circuit which makes lights glow and buzzers buzz. The circuit switches on and off in an instant as the ball moves around, making pinball a very fast-moving and exciting game.

Thick and thin

Electricity can flow through any metal wires in a circuit. But it finds it easier to flow through thick wires than thin ones. The amount of electricity flowing through a wire is called the current. If you use a thinner wire, a battery finds it harder to push electricity through it so it will produce a smaller current.

Dim the light

See what happens to your bulb when you put a really thin wire in this circuit.

What happens to the bulb as the wire gets thinner?

YOU WILL NEED
15
- A SMALL TORCH BULB (WITH A MAXIMUM VOLTAGE OF 3V OR 4.5V)
- 1.5V AA-SIZE BATTERY
- TWO INSULATED WIRES
- A PIECE OF WIRE WOOL
- STICKY TAPE

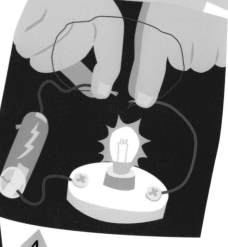

1 Follow the steps in 'Bridge the gap' (page 11) to build a circuit that makes a bulb glow when you press down a paper clip.

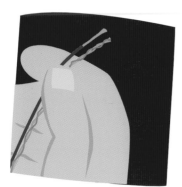

2 Pull and twist some wire wool to form a strand about 6cm long. Make this strand about the same thickness as your insulated wires.

3 Use your wire wool strand, instead of a paper clip, to bridge the gap in your circuit. Check the bulb glows.

4 Take away about three-quarters of your wire wool to make a strand that's just as long but much thinner. Use it to bridge the gap again. How does your bulb look now?

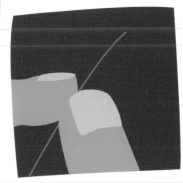

5 Make your strand even thinner. How does this affect the bulb?

What's going on?

Electricity finds it hard to flow through a circuit that contains a thin strand of wire wool. Your battery can only make a small current in a circuit like this so the bulb glows dimly. When you use an even thinner strand, the battery makes an even smaller current so the bulb glows even more dimly.

Short cut

The wires in this experiment could get warm – so ask an adult to help. Follow the steps in 'Bright idea' (page 10) to build a circuit that makes a bulb glow. Ask an adult to strip the ends of an extra wire. Then touch the bare ends of this wire against the terminals of your battery. Make sure you touch both terminals at once. What happens to the bulb?

YOU WILL NEED

15

◆ A SMALL TORCH BULB (WITH A MAXIMUM VOLTAGE OF 3V OR 4.5V)
◆ A 1.5V AA-SIZE BATTERY
◆ THREE INSULATED WIRES
◆ STICKY TAPE

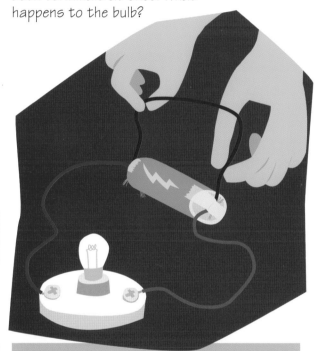

What's going on?

When you put an extra wire across the terminals of your battery, the bulb goes out. Electricity flows through your extra wire, completely by-passing the bulb. If you look closely at your lightbulb, you can see why. Inside the bulb, there's just a thin coil of metal, called a filament, which carries any electricity. Your extra wire is much thicker than this filament, so electricity flows through it far more easily. Your extra wire is a short circuit – an easier route for electric current to take.

Getting warmer

Try 'Dim the light' (far left) again, using only a couple of thin strands of wire wool. Leave the bulb glowing very dimly for at least a minute then feel the wire wool. What do you notice?

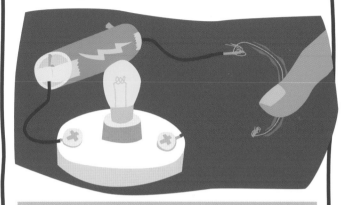

What's going on?

Because electricity finds it very hard to flow through a very thin strand of wire wool, it turns into a different form of energy – heat. This heat makes the wire wool feel slightly warmer to the touch.

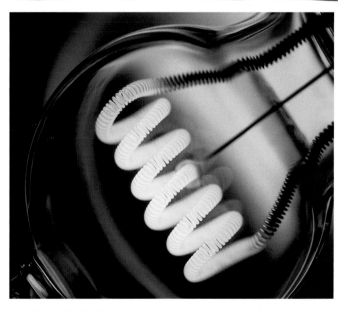

WARM GLOW
A lightbulb can turn electricity into light because it contains a very thin filament. The electricity finds it very hard to flow though the filament, so it turns into heat which makes the filament glow white-hot. This is how the bulb makes light.

Go with the flow

Electricity can flow through some substances more easily than others.
It can flow very easily through substances called 'conductors', for
instance parts made of metal. An 'insulator' is a substance
that makes it practically impossible for electricity to flow.
Plastics are usually good insulators.

The right stuff?

Here's a handy way to tell
apart some everyday
conductors and insulators.

YOU WILL NEED

15

- A SMALL TORCH BULB
  (WITH A MAXIMUM VOLTAGE
  OF 3V OR 4.5V)
- A 1.5V AA-SIZE BATTERY
- TWO INSULATED WIRES
- A METAL PAPER CLIP
- STICKY TAPE
- OBJECTS MADE OF DIFFERENT
  MATERIALS EG AN ERASER,
  A COIN, A WOODEN SPOON,
  A GLASS TUMBLER,
  A SHEET OF PAPER,
  A PLASTIC BALLPOINT PEN,
  A CHINA CUP.

1 Follow the
steps in 'Bridge
the gap' (page 11)
to make a circuit
with a break in it.
Check the bulb
glows when you
bridge the break
with a paper clip.

What's going on?

The bulb glows when you put some objects, such as the
metal coin, in the circuit. This is because these objects are
conductors. It does not glow when you put other objects,
such as the pencil eraser, in the circuit. This is because
they are insulators. Conductors, unlike insulators, are
made of materials that let electrons flow through them
readily. This why they let current flow so easily.

2 Replace the paper clip with another
object, for instance a wooden spoon. Does
the bulb glow now? Repeat with each of
your other objects in turn. Which ones
make the bulb glow and which ones don't?

Water and air

You can test two very special substances to see whether they conduct electricity – water and air. To test water, dip your two wires into a small, water-filled saucer. To test air, simply hold your two wires up in the air.

Does water conduct electricity? What about air?

YOU WILL NEED

10

◆ A SMALL TORCH BULB (WITH A MAXIMUM VOLTAGE OF 3V OR 4.5V)
◆ A 1.5V AA-SIZE BATTERY
◆ TWO INSULATED WIRES
◆ STICKY TAPE
◆ A SAUCER OF WATER

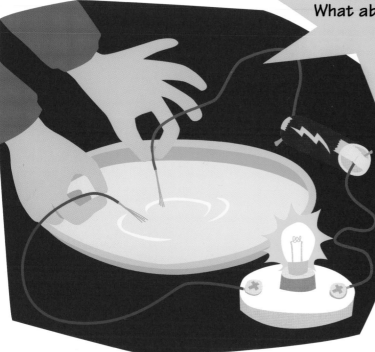

What's going on?

The bulb glows when you bridge the gap in your circuit with water – but not when you bridge it with air. Water, just like metal, lets electricity flow through it. In other words, it's a conductor. Air, on the other hand, is an insulator. Sometimes though, for instance when it is far more powerful, electricity can flow through air. Electricity flows though air to make lightning, for example. You can make enough harmless static electricity to jump a short distance through the air in 'It's alive!' (page 8).

BIRDS ON A WIRE

There is enough current running through this wire to kill. Birds can fly on to the wire and sit on it safely, though, as almost all the current flows through the wire, not the birds. This is because the wire is a much better conductor of electricity than the birds. Never try this yourself. If you reach out to a bare wire, electricity could flow through the wire, through your body and into the ground, and kill you.

Power house

A battery is a mini electricity store. When you put it in a circuit, it gradually releases the electrical energy stored inside it. This energy pushes a stream of electrons around the circuit, making an electric current. Believe it or not, you can actually make your own electricity stores, just like batteries, from a few coins and some supplies from the kitchen.

Animal electricity

Frogs' legs, not lemons, were used to make the first battery. In a very gory experiment in 1791, the scientist Luigi Galvani noticed the legs of dead frogs twitched when he touched them with two different metals. Another scientist, Alessandro Volta, used this discovery to make a battery from metal discs soaked in salty water.

Fruity tingle

Make enough electricity from a lemon to feel a tingle on your tongue!

YOU WILL NEED
- TWO COINS MADE OF DIFFERENT MATERIALS (TRY A 10p AND 2p)
- A LEMON
- A KITCHEN KNIFE (ASK AN ADULT FOR THIS)

5

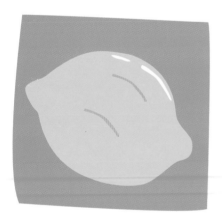

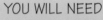

1 Ask an adult to cut two small slits in your lemon with a kitchen knife. The slits should be a few centimetres apart and long enough to hold your coins.

2 Now ask your adult helper to strip about 2cm off the ends of your insulated wires. Push a bare end of one wire into each slit. Push a coin into each slit to hold the wires in place. Make sure your coins are made of two different metals.

3 Put the loose end of each wire on your tongue, making sure the wires don't touch. Can you feel anything?

Change the recipe

Lemons aren't the only fruit that will make electricity. Try 'Fruity tingle' (left) again with other types of fruit and vegetables. Change your metal coins too. If you run out of different coins to try, use nails instead. Which home-made battery makes the biggest tingle?

What types of fruit or vegetable make the best batteries?

What's going on?

Many combinations of fruit or vegetables and metal will work as mini-batteries. You need to use a food that is acidic (potatoes and pineapples are good) along with two different metals. Some combinations produce a much bigger tingle than others.

4 Pull one wire out of the fruit then repeat step 3 What do you feel now?

What's going on?

Your lemon and coins make a simple battery. They can't produce enough electricity to power a lightbulb, but they should make enough for you to feel a tingle on your tongue. If you pull out one wire, you break the circuit so you don't feel the tingle any more. Inside a real battery, there are two plates made of different metals, just like your coins. These are separated by a type of chemical called an acid, just like the juice of your lemon.

A LIFEJACKET
As soon as this sailor falls into the sea, the salt-water fills a hollow salt-water battery on his lifejacket. This makes the battery work, switching on an emergency light so that the sailor can be seen by rescue teams.

The big push

A battery has to push electricity all the way around a circuit. If a circuit has lots of parts that make it difficult for electricity to flow, the current the battery makes will be very small. This would happen, for instance, if the circuit contained lots of skinny wires. To produce more current in the same circuit, you would need to use a battery that can give electrons a bigger push. The electrical 'push' of a battery is measured in 'volts' (V). A 9V battery, for example, has six times the push of a 1.5V battery.

Does a 9V battery make the bulbs any brighter?

Party lights

See what happens when a battery has to push current through more than one bulb.

YOU WILL NEED   15
- A 1.5 VOLT AA-SIZED BATTERY
- A 9V BATTERY
- UP TO FIVE SMALL TORCH BULBS (EACH WITH A MAXIMUM VOLTAGE OF 3V OR 4.5V)
- UP TO SIX WIRES
- STICKY TAPE

1 Follow the steps in 'Bright idea' (page 10) to make a bulb glow. Check the bulb is glowing and try to remember how bright it looks.

2 Add another bulb to the circuit, like this. Do both bulbs glow? How bright are they?

3 Add more lightbulbs to the circuit. What happens to their brightness? Do they always glow?

4 While you have three or more bulbs in the circuit, swap your battery for a 9V one and see what happens.

What's going on?

As you put more bulbs in this circuit, each one gets dimmer. That's because the bulbs have to share the battery's voltage. The battery has to use some of its voltage to push electricity through each bulb. The current in the circuit reduces every time a bulb is added. If lots of bulbs are added, the current becomes so low, it can't make the bulbs glow at all. A 9V battery pushes more current around the circuit so it can make more bulbs glow.

Dimmer switch

Follow the steps in 'Bridge the gap' (page 11) to make a broken circuit. Bridge the gap in the circuit with a soft propelling pencil lead. Does the bulb glow?

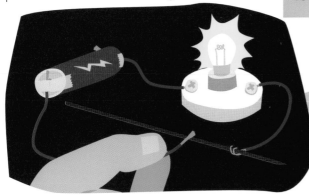

What happens if you vary the length of the lead between the wires?

What's going on?

As you vary the length of pencil lead between the wires, you change the brightness of the bulb. That's because electricity finds it hard to flow through the lead. The longer the lead is, the more voltage the battery needs to push electricity through it. This leaves less voltage to make the bulb glow.

String them out

Follow steps 1 and 2 of 'Party lights' (far left) to light up two bulbs. Now replace your wires with very long ones. Does this change the brightness of the bulbs?

What's going on?

When you make the wires in your circuit longer, the brightness of the bulbs hardly changes at all. That's because electricity finds it very easy to flow through the wires. No matter how long the wires are, very little of the battery's voltage is used to push electricity through them.

ELECTRIC GUITAR

The volume knob on this electric guitar works just like your dimmer switch. When you turn it, you move two wires nearer and further apart, along a piece of graphite (the material that makes up a pencil lead). This varies the voltage that is available for the amplifier and loudspeaker. When they get more voltage, they make a louder sound.

Neat work

Circuits don't have to be thick and bulky. In fact, you can make a circuit that has wires as thin as a sheet of paper.

A circuit like this can be squeezed into the tightest of spaces – for instance inside a personal stereo or a computer.

Circuit board

Using kitchen foil, you can make a really flat circuit that you can turn into an exciting picture!

YOU WILL NEED **20**
- ◆ A SHEET OF BAKING FOIL
- ◆ A STIFF PIECE OF CARDBOARD (ABOUT 15CM X 20CM)
- ◆ A 9V BATTERY
- ◆ TWO SMALL LIGHTBULBS (WITH A MAXIMUM VOLTAGE OF 3V OR 4.5V)
- ◆ GLUE AND STICKY TAPE
- ◆ SHORT INSULATED WIRES
- ◆ SCISSORS

Mini marvels

Computers changed enormously from the mid 1970s, when the first 'microchips' were sold. No bigger than a postage stamp, each chip contained thousands of wires, etched on to a slither of silicon. Before chips, the computers were made of bulky circuits so they were expensive and huge. A machine with no more computing power than a modern hand-held computer toy took up as much space as several wardrobes!

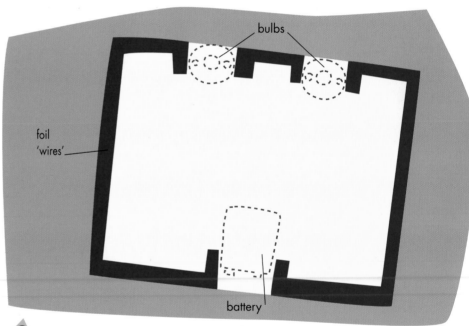

bulbs

foil 'wires'

battery

1 Cut out some neat strips of baking foil, about 2cm wide and 15cm long.

2 Draw this pattern on to the piece of cardboard. This is the design for your circuit.

What conducts the electricity in your circuit board?

3 Stick strips of foil over the parts of the design that are wires.

Glowing masterpiece

Make some holes in the sheet of paper so that when you place it on your circuit the lightbulbs will poke through. Design a colourful picture that will make use of your bulbs, then stick it on to your circuit. Keep the bulbs in place with some re-usable adhesive. When you've finished, stand back and admire your glowing masterpiece!

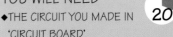

What's going on?

Your circuit is so flat, you have been able to stick it on to the back of a picture. If you like, make a paper clip switch between the battery and circuit board so you can turn your picture on and off as you please (see page 11 for some clues on how to do this).

4 Using short lengths of real wire and some sticky tape, connect your two bulbs and battery to the foil strips. Check your lightbulbs glow.

What's going on?

You have made a very flat circuit by replacing ordinary wires with strips of baking foil. The baking foil conducts electricity just like an ordinary wire. The cardboard backing makes the circuit more robust and helps to keep everything in place.

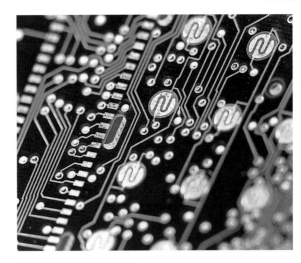

LOOK! NO WIRES

This 'printed circuit board' comes from the inside of a TV remote control. Gadgets like this have very few ordinary wires as most of their circuits look like this. The wires of the circuit, stuck on to the backing, aren't much thicker than a layer of paint.

Branching out

A circuit doesn't have to be made in just one loop. Sometimes, it's handy to give it two or more separate branches. When parts of a circuit are connected in the same loop, they are 'in series'. When they are in two separate loops, connected side by side, they are 'in parallel'. When bulbs are wired in parallel, it's easy to switch them on and off independently of one another.

Ladder of lights

See what happens when you link bulbs together like the rungs of a ladder, in parallel.

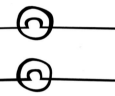

YOU WILL NEED

15

- A 1.5V AA-SIZED BATTERY
- TWO SMALL TORCH BULBS (WITH A MAXIMUM VOLTAGE OF 3V OR 4.5V)
- TWO SHORT WIRES
- TWO LONG WIRES
- STICKY TAPE
- SCISSORS

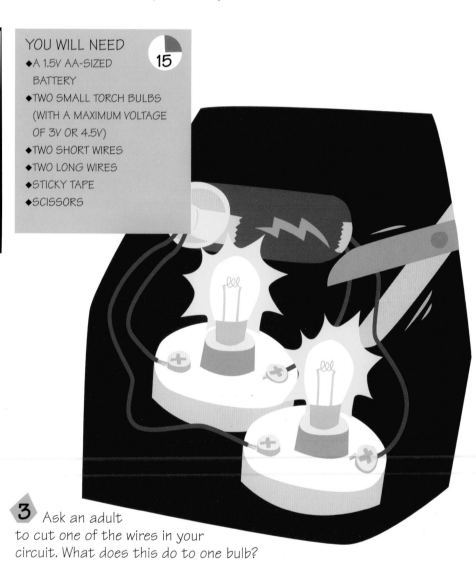

1 Follow the steps in 'Bright idea' (page 10) to light up a bulb. Use quite short wires to connect the bulb to the battery. Check that the bulb is glowing.

2 Using two slightly longer wires, connect another lightbulb across the terminals of the battery. Do both lightbulbs glow?

3 Ask an adult to cut one of the wires in your circuit. What does this do to one bulb?

What's going on?

This circuit makes both the bulbs glow. That's because each bulb is in its own complete loop. The two bulbs are wired in parallel. Electricity can flow through both loops at the same time. It goes out of the battery, through the bulbs, then back into the battery again. When you cut a wire connecting one bulb to the battery, you turn that bulb off. However, you haven't broken the other bulb's loop, so that one continues glowing.

Upstairs, downstairs

Follow steps 1 to 3 of 'Ladder of lights' (left) to make a circuit that lights two bulbs in parallel. Now break a wire connecting each bulb to the battery. Bridge the gap in each loop of your circuit with a paper clip. Page 11 shows you how to do this.

YOU WILL NEED
- A 1.5V AA-SIZED BATTERY
- TWO SMALL TORCH BULBS (WITH A MAXIMUM VOLTAGE OF 3V OR 4.5V
- TWO SHORT WIRES
- TWO LONG WIRES
- TWO PAPER CLIPS
- STICKY TAPE

15

Can you use the paper clips to turn your lights on and off?

What's going on?
You can switch on either bulb, without affecting the other one, simply by pressing down the paper clip switch that's wired to that bulb. That's because the bulbs are wired in parallel. Each of the paper clip switches is wired in series with one of the bulbs.

FLASHBACK

First fairies
The first fairy lights went on sale at the end of the nineteenth century. Unlike fairy lights today, which are strung together in series, these were wired in parallel. This 'failsafe' was important because the early bulbs frequently broke. When one bulb stopped working, the others would carry on glowing.

SKYSCRAPER
Towering over 40 stories high, this skyscraper is illuminated by thousands of lights that are connected in parallel. The lights on each floor make a different branch of a large parallel circuit. When security guards patrol the building at night, they can switch on one branch of the circuit at a time. This makes the lights glow on just one floor, saving electricity.

Feel the force

Magnets vary widely in size, shape and strength, but they can all do two very special things – they can pull objects made of iron or nickel towards them, and they can also attract or repel other magnets. Some magnets occur naturally. They have special magnetic properties as soon as they are mined from the ground. Others are specially made from non-magnets, for instance using electricity. Materials like iron and nickel that are attracted towards a magnet are called 'magnetic materials'.

Jump to it!

Next time someone drops some pins, help them to pick them up with a magnet!

YOU WILL NEED
- ◆ A MAGNET
- ◆ STEEL PINS

5

Where do most of the pins stick to the magnet?

2 Try to pick up a chain of pins with the magnet. How many pins can you pick up this way?

3 Put one pin on the table then gradually move the magnet closer to it. What happens?

1 Bring your magnet close to a small pile of loose pins. Can you pick up the pins with your magnet?

What's going on?

Pins stick to the magnet because they are made of steel, a material that contains lots of iron. They are pulled towards it if they are nearby. The magnet pulls most strongly at its ends so that is where most of the pins will stick. Scientists call the ends of the magnet its 'poles'. When a pin sticks to the magnet, it becomes part of the magnet so it can pick up more pins itself. That's why you can pick up a chain of pins.

Is it magnetic?

You can find out which materials are magnetic by trying to pick up a few different objects around your home. (Warning: magnets damage floppy discs, tapes, TVs and computers, so keep them away from these!)

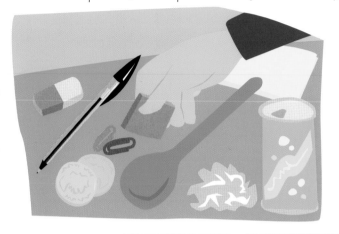

What's going on?

Only objects that contain iron or nickel are attracted to the magnet. You may have found these materials in some of the coins or keys that you tested. The magnet has no effect on objects such as the wooden spoon and pencil eraser because these don't contain any iron or nickel. For the same reason it has no effect on the baking foil – it's made of aluminium.

Can sorter

You can use your magnet to sort steel and aluminium cans for recycling. Using the string and sticky tape, dangle your magnet from the bottom of a chair. Make sure the magnet is about 10cm above the ground. Roll your cans under the magnet, one at a time. Do all the cans roll past the magnet smoothly?

What's going on?

The aluminium cans roll straight past the magnet, but the steel cans slow down. They may even stop moving completely or stick to the magnet. This is because steel is a magnetic material. At refuse centres, cans are often sorted by moving them on a conveyor belt past a line of magnets.

HIGH FLYER

Tilting up and down to steer the plane, this aeroplane wing flap is controlled by a motor that uses a special magnet. Most magnets are mainly made of iron but this one contains lots of boron, a rare metal. This makes it much more powerful than an ordinary magnet. Only a tiny boron magnet is needed to move the wing flap. This keeps the wing as light as possible.

Pole to pole

Every magnet has two distinct poles. To tell them apart, we call them 'north' or 'south' – you can find out more about this on page 34. The area of force around a magnet is called its 'magnetic field'. You can use magnets to create some funny effects!

Opposites attract

The forces between the poles of two magnets can be surprisingly strong – strong enough for you to feel them.

YOU WILL NEED
◆ A RULER
◆ A PENCIL
◆ TWO BAR MAGNETS

5

When do the forces between the magnets feel the strongest?

1 Take a close look at your two bar magnets. There should be paint marks on their ends to tell you which pole is which. They may be labelled 'north' or 'south'. Or they may simply be painted different colours.

2 Bring two opposite poles of your two magnets close together. Can you feel the force that pulls them together?

3 Turn one of your magnets around so two like poles are facing each other. What force can you feel now? Hold the magnets 3cm apart, then 6cm, then 9cm. How close do the magnets have to be to make a force you can feel?

What's going on?

You feel a strong force between your two magnets when you bring them close together. When different poles are facing, this force attracts the magnets towards each other. When the same poles face each other, this force repels them (pushes them apart). The force gets weaker as the magnets get further apart.

Dancing socks

Put a magnet inside each sock and dangle the socks in the air. Move the socks close together and watch them dance around! Pad the socks out by wrapping each magnet in a couple of layers of paper. Does the trick still work? Now put several layers of paper around the magnets.

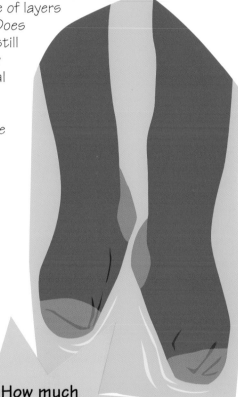

How much paper can you put round the magnets before the trick stops working?

What's going on?

Unless your magnets are very weak, they will be able to attract or repel each other, even though they are covered by your socks. A couple of layers of paper won't weaken the forces between them very much but several layers of paper will. The stronger your magnets, the more paper you can wrap round them before the socks will stop dancing.

Spider stealth

Draw a spider about 5cm across and cut it out. Now tape a paper clip to the bottom of your spider and put it on to the sheet of card. You can make it move wherever you want using a magnet hidden underneath the card!

What's going on?

If your magnet is strong enough, it will pull the paper clip towards it, even though it's separated from it by the card. Anyone watching will see the spider move around in a most mysterious way!

OFF THE RAILS

Magnetic forces between runners on the bottom of the train and the track make this train hover and move forwards. Called a Maglev, the train never touches the rails below it. It travels far more smoothly and quietly than an ordinary train.

Magnetic art

Magnets aren't only useful for making machines and tools. With a little imagination, you can also use them to create magnetic works of art! You can make interesting moving sculptures, like the one below, or fascinating permanent pictures of a magnet's forces.

Freaky pendulum

Three magnets will make this sculpture that swings in the strangest of ways.

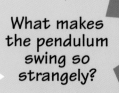

What makes the pendulum swing so strangely?

YOU WILL NEED

10

- THREE MAGNETS
- AN IRON NAIL
- STRING
- A CHAIR
- MODELLING CLAY
- STICKY TAPE

1 Tie some string to the head of your nail. Then dangle the nail from a rung under the chair. Make sure one of your magnets can fit underneath your hanging nail, with a gap of about 1cm.

2 Tap the nail gently and watch it swing to and fro like a pendulum. Make sure there are no magnets near your nail when you do this.

3 Using some modelling clay, fix three magnets to the floor, like this. Make sure the same poles of the magnets are facing each other. The poles should be about 2cm apart.

4 Move the chair so the nail is directly over the centre of the magnets. Then gently tap the nail again. What happens?

What's going on?

When there are no magnets around, the nail swings to and fro smoothly, just like the pendulum of an old-fashioned clock. The only force the nail feels is the force of gravity. When you put the magnets beneath the nail, it swings in a crazy, unpredictable manner. This is because it also feels a force from each of the magnets. As it swings nearer and further from each magnet, the force on it varies continually.

Get the picture

Place your magnet under a sheet of paper. Sprinkle iron filings on the paper. The filings will form a definite pattern because the magnet is under the paper. Put a little paint on your toothbrush then flick the toothbrush with your finger to spray paint on to the paper. When the paint is dry, carefully remove the magnet and filings.

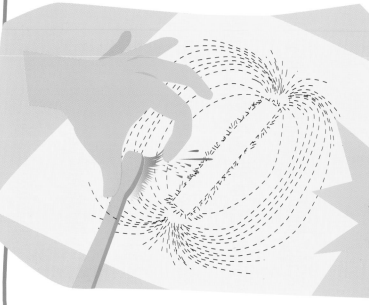

Where do most of the filings settle?

What's going on?

Most filings settle around the poles because this is where the force of the magnet is greatest. Others settle in onion-shaped rings around the magnet. These rings are called 'lines of force'. The pattern of the filings is perfectly symmetrical because the magnet creates exactly the same force at each pole and on each side.

FLASHBACK

Flea circus

Some tricksters in the nineteenth century pretended they had performing fleas. They would entertain people with their flea circuses at theatres and fairgrounds. The tricksters pulled strings and moved tiny metal props around with hidden magnets. This made it look as if the circus contained a team of flea acrobats.

THUNDERBIRD PUPPET
This original Thunderbirds puppet, Scott, has a pair of magnets in his lips. Scott's mouth is normally held closed by a spring, but when his magnets are activated, they create a force which pushes his lips apart so he can 'speak'.

Make your own magnets

Every magnet is made of billions of tiny ones, called 'domains', that are all lined up in the same direction. Other materials have domains too but theirs are all in a jumble. If you have a magnet, you can tease the domains of magnetic materials to make them face the same way. In this way, you can make more magnets of your own.

At a stroke

To turn a paper clip into a magnet, you just have to stroke it the right way.

YOU WILL NEED ⏱ **10**
- ◆ TWO STEEL PAPER CLIPS
- ◆ A MAGNET
- ◆ MODELLING CLAY

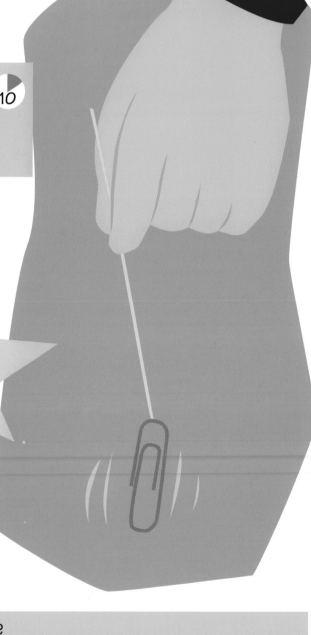

1 Unfurl a steel paper clip and lay it on a firm surface. Fix it in place with some modelling clay.

What makes the paper clip turn into a magnet?

3 Move your magnet out of the way, pick up your steel paper clip and test it. Can you pick up another paper clip with it?

2 Holding your bar magnet in one hand, move it through the air in a loop like this, close to the paper clip. Repeat this several times. Take care to keep your magnet facing the same way. Never change the direction of the loop.

What's going on?

When you stroke your steel paper clip with a magnet, you turn the paper clip into a magnet too. This is because the magnet pulls at the domains of the paper clip until they all face in one direction. The magnet can move the domains around because the domains themselves are microscopic magnets.

Magnetic mobile

YOU WILL NEED
◆ A MAGNET
◆ SOME STRING AND A SELECTION OF LIGHTWEIGHT IRON AND STEEL OBJECTS EG STEEL PAPER CLIPS, IRON NAIL AND OLD STEEL KEY.

20

Make a magnetic mobile and see how long it lasts. Follow the steps in 'At a stroke' (left) to magnetise lots of things. Suspend your largest object from a piece of string just above floor level, then link together as many of the other objects as you can. Be careful when using nails in this experiment. Keep the items together using the magnetic forces between them – don't use sticky tape or glue. Check your mobile to see what happens.

What makes magnetism fade over time?

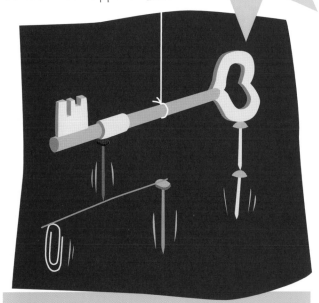

What's going on?
As every part of this mobile is a magnet, you can keep it together without any glue or sticky tape. Over time, the magnetism of your objects will fade. This happens faster if the mobile gets bashed or dropped. Every small shock to the mobile jumbles up its domains a little. This reduces its magnetism. Steel objects stay magnetic far longer than iron objects because their domains are harder to jumble.

FLASHBACK

Off the menu
Hundreds of years ago, onions and garlic were banned from many ships' rations. Ships navigated using magnetic compasses (see page 34) and crews mistakenly believed that onions and garlic affected magnets! The sailors worried that they would lose their way if the ship's compasses became confused.

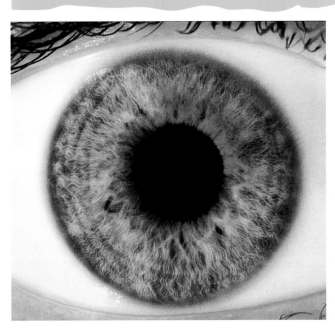

EYE FULL
Magnets can be used to remove some metal objects safely from the eye. The metal can be removed without touching the eye so the eye is far less likely to be damaged. Surgeons usually magnify an eye before they perform the delicate task of pulling any object from it.

Mini-magnets

You can't destroy a magnet just by chopping it in half. That's because the two halves of magnet you are left with will both still have billions of domains that all point in the same direction. These domains will give both halves their magnetism.

Double up

Ask an adult to help you chop a home-made magnet in half – and you'll have two home-made mini-magnets!

YOU WILL NEED
- ◆TWO STEEL PAPER CLIPS
- ◆A MAGNET
- ◆COTTON THREAD
- ◆WIRE CLIPPERS OR PLIERS (ASK AN ADULT FOR THESE)

15

1 Follow the instructions in 'At a stroke' (see page 30) to turn a paper clip into a home-made magnet. Check your home-made magnet works.

2 Ask an adult to chop your home-made magnet in half, using wire clippers or pliers.

How does cutting a magnet in half make two magnets?

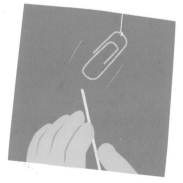

3 Dangle an ordinary metal paper clip from a cotton thread. Hold one half of your broken home-made magnet close to it. Does it attract the paper clip? Repeat this step using the other half of your home-made magnet.

4 Now dangle one half of your broken magnet from another cotton thread. Hold the other half close to it. Can you make the two halves attract each other? What happens if you turn around the half of the magnet that's in your hand?

What's going on?

When you chopped your home-made magnet in half, you made two mini-magnets. That's because each half still has large numbers of domains all facing in the same direction. Each mini-magnet can attract a paper clip. As it has a north and south pole, it can also attract and repel the other mini-magnet. You can cut your home-made magnet into more pieces to make even smaller magnets.

Wipe out

Play an unwanted music tape and stop it about half way through. Take the tape out of the tape player and pull out a loop of tape about 30cm long. Pass a magnet close to the end of the loop of tape. Be careful not to bring it close to the rest of the audio tape. Carefully wind the loop back into the tape then play the tape again. What happens when you reach the part of the tape that was near the magnet?

YOU WILL NEED | 10
◆ AN UNWANTED AUDIO TAPE WITH MUSIC RECORDED ON IT (ASK AN ADULT'S PERMISSION FIRST!)
◆ A TAPE PLAYER
◆ A MAGNET

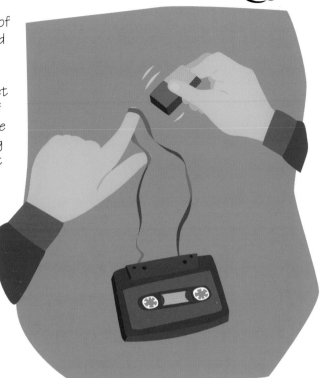

What's going on?

The magnet wiped the sound from part of the tape. Small groups of magnetic granules on the tape store tiny fragments of sound. Each fragment is less than a ten-thousandth of a second long. The granuales have stronger magnetism when a louder sound is stored. When you pass a magnet close to the tape, you overpower the magnetism of each group of granules, wiping out this stored information.

FLASHBACK

Danger music

Playing some of the first magnetic recordings, in the 1930s, was a dangerous business. Rather than using magnetic granules on tape, people stored sound on a piece of magnetised wire. To play back the sound, the wire had to move through a machine at high speed. If the wire snapped, it could break loose, cutting through anything – or anyone – in the area. Listeners had to be ready to make a speedy exit!

COMPUTER HARD DISK
The hard disk in your computer uses magnetism to store words, pictures and other information. Tiny magnets change the pattern of the magnetism to store information as you work, or to wipe it off.

Map it out

Ever since people discovered magnets, they have used them to find their way from place to place. Magnets can be used to navigate because they always turn around to face roughly north. This is because they are affected by the Earth, which itself acts like a very big but weak magnet. A magnet used to find north is called a 'compass'.

Travelling light

This compass, which can fit in a matchbox, is also light enough to float on water.

YOU WILL NEED
- A MAGNET   15
- A STEEL PIN
- A BOTTLE CORK
- MODELLING CLAY
- A LARGE PLASTIC BOWL
- WATER
- A CRAFT KNIFE
  (ASK AN ADULT)

1 Follow the instructions in 'At a stroke' (page 30) to turn a steel pin into a magnet. Use your magnet to do this.

2 Ask an adult to cut a small disk, about 1cm thick, from the end of your bottle cork using the craft knife. Place the pin on top of the cork. Fix it in place with a tiny amount of modelling clay.

What happens to the pin when you turn the bowl?

3 Fill the bowl with water. Then carefully float the steel pin and cork in it.

Stone followers

Magnetite, a type of iron, is a naturally occurring magnet. Tiny fragments of magnetite are often called lodestones, meaning 'leading stones'. They are called this because they can be used to point north, leading the way home. The Chinese were the first to discover that lodestones could be used to navigate. They used lodestones to make the first compasses around 2,300 years ago.

About turn

You can confuse your compass with a magnet. Follow the steps in 'Travelling light' (left) to make a mini, floating compass. Check it points in a north–south direction when it settles. Then bring a magnet a few centimetres away from your compass. What happens?

How can a magnet confuse a compass?

20

What's going on?

As soon as you bring a magnet close to your compass, the compass' poles spin towards the magnet's poles, so the compass stops pointing north. That's because your magnet is much stronger than the Earth's magnetism. The magnet overpowers the Earth's magnetism, confusing the compass.

4 Wait for the steel pin and cork to stop turning. Draw a picture of the pin on a piece of paper. Lie it on the floor and note which way the needle faces.

What's going on?

When it stops turning, the magnetised steel pin always lies in the same direction, even if you turn the bowl. That direction is roughly north–south. It does this because its north and south poles are being attracted by the Earth, which itself is a giant, weak magnet. One pole of the Earth's magnetism is roughly north on the map. The other is roughly south.

PIGEON POST

With an amazing sense of direction, pigeons like this can find their way home even after they are moved hundreds of kilometres away. Scientists think homing pigeons are good navigators partly because they can sense the Earth's magnetism.

Pick-up power

Electricity and magnetism are very closely linked. When electricity flows through a wire, it turns the wire into a magnet. Coiled wire concentrates this magnetism so that it is strong enough to pick things up. When you move a magnet near a wire, you make a tiny current. Our homes are full of machines that make use of this connection between electricity and magnetism. We call the link between electricity and magnetism 'electromagnetism'.

Electric magnet

Send electricity through a coil of wire to make a strong magnet. The wires in this experiment could get warm – ask an adult for help.

YOU WILL NEED
- AN IRON NAIL
- A VERY LONG WIRE WITH PLASTIC COATING
- A PAPER CLIP
- A 9V BATTERY
- STICKY TAPE
- STEEL PINS

15

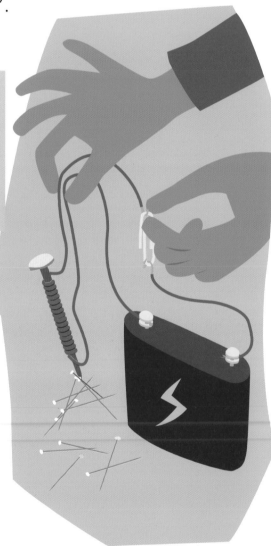

How can an iron nail be turned into a magnet?

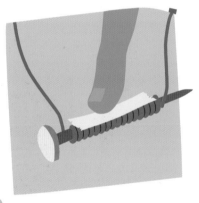

1 Wind the wire tightly around the iron nail at least ten times, holding it in place with sticky tape.

3 Hold the nail over a pile of steel pins. What happens? Remove the paper clip switch to turn the circuit off. What happens now?

2 Connect one end of the wire around your nail to a terminal of your 9V battery. Connect the other end to the other terminal, and add a paper clip switch (see page 11).

What's going on?

When the switch is in place, the iron nail picks up pins. That's because electricity flows through the circuit, turning its wires into weak magnets. As part of the wire is coiled, it concentrates this magnetism. It makes a strong enough magnetic force to turn the nail into a magnet. A magnet like this, that only works when electricity flows around it, is called an 'electromagnet'.

Electric eels

Follow the steps in 'Electric magnet' (left) to make an electromagnet. Then use it to challenge a friend to a game of electric eels. Cut out some eels from tissue paper then stick a tiny piece of wire wool to their heads. Take turns to pick up eels, against the clock, using nothing but your electromagnet. You'll need to use all your skill to turn your electromagnet on and off at the right time. If you pick up one eel, you can keep it. If you pick up two or more, you have to throw them back!

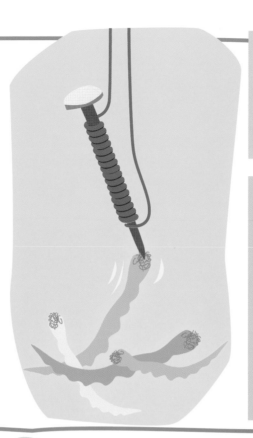

YOU WILL NEED

25

◆ THE ELECTROMAGNET MADE IN 'ELECTRIC MAGNET'
◆ TISSUE PAPER
◆ WIRE WOOL
◆ STICKY TAPE

What's going on?

As all the eels have wire wool on their heads, you're able to pick them up with your electromagnet. The nail is only magnetised when the paper clip switch is on. When the clip is switched off, there is no electric current running through the circuit, so there is no magnetism.

FLASHBACK

Moving idea

When the scientist, Michael Faraday, demonstrated the first motor in 1821, he had some trouble convincing people 'electromagnetism' would be so useful. Nowadays, the link between electricity and magnetism enables us to build all sorts of machines that use electricity to control how things move. An electric motor and loudspeaker are just a couple of examples.

AT THE SCRAP YARD

Dumps and scrap yards often have huge cranes that carry electromagnets, just like this. These are strong enough to pick up huge lumps of metal – even whole cars.

Glossary

Attract Two things attract each other if they want to pull themselves closer together. This happens when they have opposite electrical charges (when one has too many electrons and the other has too few). A magnet will attract objects that contain lots of iron or nickel. Two magnets will attract each other if the north pole of one is close to the south pole of the other.

Charge Something has charge if it has too many or too few electrons. This could happen because you've rubbed it with another object to make static electricity. Two objects have the same type of charge if they've both lost electrons of if they've both gained them. They have 'opposite' charges if one has gained electrons but the other has lost them.

Compass A device that can be used to find out roughly where north is. The most important part of a compass is the pointer, which is a magnet. Like all magnets, the pointer will end up lying in a roughly north–south direction when it's left to swing freely.

Conductor A substance that electricity can flow through easily. Metal and water are both good conductors. These are the raw materials of many electrical devices, for instance wires, switches and lightbulbs. You may also come across the word 'conductor' when people are talking about things other than electricity. For instance, engineers often ask if a material is a good conductor of heat.

Current A measure of how much electricity is flowing. Current is measured in amps (A). A circuit will have a bigger current if a battery finds it easier to push electricity around it. A larger current means more electrons are flowing through the circuit.

Domains The millions of mini-magnets, far too tiny to see, that make up every material.

The domains of a magnet all face in the same direction. Their magnetism will fade if their domains get jumbled, for instance because they have been bashed with a hammer.

Electricity The form of energy that makes toasters, house lights, televisions and all other electrical things work. Electricity is created by particles, called electrons, which are far too tiny to see. Electrons make 'current electricity' when they flow through things such as wires and lightbulbs. When they are not moving, electrons make 'static electricity'.

Electromagnet A magnet that only works when electricity flows through it. Most electromagnets are made of a coil of wire, wrapped around some metal to boost its magnetic strength.

Electron A tiny particle that is far too tiny to see. There are one or more electrons in every atom. When electrons flow through things, for instance a wire, they make current electricity. When they rub off one thing and on to another, they make static electricity.

Filament The thin, coiled wire inside a lightbulb that makes the bulb glow. Electricity finds it hard to flow through this wire so it turns into another form of energy, heat. This makes the filament glow white hot, producing light.

Insulator A substance that makes it very hard for electricity to flow. Wood, paper, glass and plastic are all good insulators. Electric machines and parts are often covered in insulators to make them safe – for instance, wires are often covered in plastic and a television is built inside a plastic box. People also use the word 'insulator' when they're not talking about electricity. For instance, they might look for a material that's a good insulator of heat.

Magnet An object that can pull iron or nickel objects towards it. Magnets can also attract or repel other magnets. Some rocks, like magnetite, are naturally occuring magnets. Other magnets can be made in the laboratory, for instance by stroking iron or nickel with other magnets.

Magnetic field The area around a magnet where it can noticeably attract or repel things. Stronger magnets have a larger magnetic field.

Magnetic materials Materials that are attracted towards magnets. Iron and nickel are magnetic materials. So are many materials that contain either of these two metals. Steel, for instance, contains lots of iron so it is a magnetic material.

Parallel The word used to describe electrical parts that have been wired into two or more separate loops. Each loop lets electricity flow out of the battery, through itself, then back into the battery again.

Poles The two areas of a magnet, usually at its ends, in which the magnet's pull is strongest. If you let a magnet swing freely, one pole will always end up pointing approximately south. This pole is the magnet's 'south pole'. The other, called the magnet's 'north pole', will always end up pointing roughly north. The poles end up pointing in these directions because they are attracted to the north and south poles of the Earth, which is itself a giant magnet.

Repel Two things repel each other if they want to push themselves further apart. This happens when they have the same type of electrical charge (when both objects have too few electrons or both have too many). Two magnets will repel each other if the north pole of one is close to the north pole of another. They will also repel if their south poles are close together.

Series The word used to describe electrical things that have been strung together in a single loop. This loop lets electricity flow out of the battery, through each part, then into the battery again.

Short circuit A very easy path that electricity can take around a circuit. A wire directly connected to the two terminals of a battery will make a short circuit. Electricity will always take a short circuit when it can.

Static electricity A type of electricity that you can make by rubbing certain things together, for instance a nylon cloth and a plastic ruler. When you do this, you brush electrons off one item and on to another. This gives both objects an electrical 'charge'.

Voltage A measure of the electrical 'push' a battery can give to the electrons flowing around a circuit. This push is measured in volts (V). Most batteries have their voltage written on their casing. A 4.5V battery, for instance, has three times the electrical push of a 1.5V battery.

Index

A B C

Acid 17
Aeroplane wing flap 25
Airship 9
Amber 6
Amplifier 19
Animal electricity 16
Art, magnetic 28–29, 31
Attraction 8–9, 26–27
Batteries
   fruit and vegetable 16–17
   home-made 16–17
   how they work 13
   using 10–11
Boron 25
Can sorter 25
Cans
   aluminium 25
   steel 25
Charge 6–7, 8–9
Circuit 10–11
Circuit board, printed 21
Compass 31, 34
Computers 20, 33
Conductors 14–15
Connections 4
Current electricity 10–11

D E

Domains, magnetic 32–33
Electric guitar 19
Electrons 7, 8, 9
Eye surgery, magnetic 31

F

Fairy lights 23
Filament 13
Flea circus 29
Foil, aluminium 20

G H

Galvani, Luigi 16
Garlic 31
Hindenburg airship 9

I J K

Insulators 14–15
Iron filings 29

L

Lifejacket 17
Light, early electric 11
Lightbulb
   how it works 13
   using 10–13
Lightning 7
Loudspeaker 19

M N O

Maglev train 27
Magnetic materials 24–25
Magnetic poles 26–27
Magnets 24–25
   making 30–33
Microchips 20
Onions 31

P

Parallel circuits 23–24
Pendulum 28
Pinball 11
   Poles, north and south 26, 34, 35

Q R

Recordings, early sound 33
Repulsion 8–9, 26–27

S

Safety 5
Series circuits
   definition 23
   making 10–15
Short circuit 13
Silicon 21
Skyscraper 23
Static electricity 6–7, 8–9

Storm, electric 7
Switch 10–11, 23

TUV

Thompson, J J 5
Thunderbirds 29
Volt 18
Volta, Alessandro 16
Voltage 18–19
Volume control 19

W X Y Z

Water 15
Wire 4, 10–11
   thickness 12–13

Picture Credits

London Features International (bottom right) 29

Science Photo Library (bottom right) 21, 33

Pictor International (bottom right) 15

PowerStock Photo Library (bottom right) 37

Telegraph Colour Library (bottom right) 11, 25

Tony Stone (bottom right) 13, 19, 23, 31, 35

Corbis (bottom right) 7, 9

Central Japan Railway Company (bottom right) 27

Royal National Lifeboat Institution (bottom right) 17